COMMUNITY HELPERS SERIES

ANNE NEIGOFF
DINNER'S READY

Pictures: Charles Lynch

ALBERT WHITMAN & COMPANY   Chicago

Picture Dictionary

cannery worker

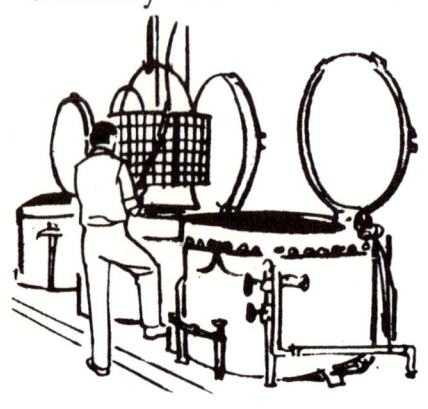

dairyman

consumer

deliveryman

cook

fisherman

ISBN 0-8075-1594-9   L.C. Card Number 76-150805
© 1971 by Albert Whitman & Company, Chicago
Published simultaneously in Canada by George J. McLeod, Limited, Toronto
Printed in the U.S.A.   All rights reserved

food inspector

orchard worker

rancher

restaurant workers

supermarket worker

test cooks

"Dinner's ready, come and get it!
Cowboy cooks call that, and so does Pete,
the cook at the Roundup Restaurant.
Tina and Ben like to eat at the Roundup,
and so do Mother and Dad.
"After teaching all day," Mother says,
"I like to let someone else cook."
"And Pete's a better cook than I am,"
Dad says.
Ben just says, "Ummm, good potatoes."

Everyone likes Pete's hamburgers.
He makes good steak sandwiches and hot dogs and chicken-in-a-basket, too.
Tom helps Pete get food ready.
He cuts pies and scoops out ice cream.
Linda carries the food to the tables.

Sally carries food to people who eat in their cars.
Inside, Bess takes money and makes change.
How clean and friendly the Roundup is!
"You all come back," Pete always calls.
"Yes, sir!" Ben always answers.

This Saturday morning Mother and Tina have a secret.
Tina has made a birthday cake.
"Wait till Dad sees that," Mother says.
"He'll be surprised."
"Help me hide it," Tina whispers.
"I hear Dad coming."
"Hurry, girls," Dad says. "Ben and I are ready to take you shopping."

Every Saturday Dad and Mother shop
at the big supermarket.
Ben and Tina go along to help.
Mother picks out the meat.
Dad gets fruits and vegetables.
Ben and Tina look for bread and cookies.

Mother and Dad are careful shoppers.
They like this supermarket.
The workers keep the food fresh and clean.
Mother shows Ben and Tina her
shopping list.
"These eggs are a good buy today,"
she says, "and so is this meat."
"What about these cookies?" asks Ben.
"They're a good buy," Mother agrees.

Mother stops to read what it says on a can. "I want to be a good consumer and know what I'm getting," she explains.
"What do you want to be?" asks Ben.
Mother laughs. "Oh, Ben," she says, "a consumer is anybody who uses things. We're all food consumers. It's important to be a good consumer and choose wisely."

Many people buy food at the supermarket.
Many workers are busy keeping the store filled with food to sell.
Deliverymen come with loads of meat, vegetables, and other good things to eat.
Men carry in milk, ice cream, and butter from the dairy truck.
Here comes the bakery truck.
The driver has cakes and pies to deliver.

Where does all the food come from?
Farmers and ranchers raise animals
used for meat.
Chickens and turkeys come from other farms.
Fishermen on oceans and lakes catch big fish
and little fish.

Peas, beans, and tomatoes grow on farms.
There are fields of sweet corn, potatoes,
pumpkins, and lettuce.
Farmers who raise these crops are
called truck gardeners.
On big farms there are wheat fields
as far as you can see.
Other crops to feed people and animals
grow on these farms, too.

Have you ever picked an apple from a tree?
Fruit trees grow in orchards — apples, peaches, and cherries.
There are groves where golden oranges grow.
There are fields of red strawberries.
Many workers pick the fruit we eat.
Many people grow the food we need.

Lettuce and melons, tomatoes and apples are good to eat just as they are.
But lots of vegetables, fruits, and meats have to be canned or frozen or packaged before they are sold in the supermarket. These foods keep for a long time.
They are easy to handle and sell.

What a busy and clean place a cannery is!
Huge pots hold more vegetables than
anyone could ever cook at home.
Workers make sure machines fill cans
just the right way.
At last the shiny cans get labels and
go into boxes, ready for store shelves.

LOUISA ELEMENTARY SCHOOL

Meat and fish, fruit and vegetables, can be
canned or frozen or smoked or dried.
They are ready to use anywhere, anytime.

How are wheat and grains used?
Wheat is sent to mills to be made into
flour for bread, rolls, cookies, and cake.
Breakfast cereals are made from corn, oats,
and rice.

Tank trucks take milk from dairy farms
to spic-and-span dairies.
Pasteurized milk is put into cartons.
It is made into butter and ice cream, too.
What flavor do you like best?

Someday you may have a new flavor of ice cream to taste.
This is because workers in special kitchens try new ways to use food.
They try to make food taste better.
They test food to make sure it is safe and good.

Food inspectors are like food detectives. They check to make sure food is clean and healthy and safe to eat.
There are government inspectors who put special marks on food they have checked. A good consumer looks for these marks.

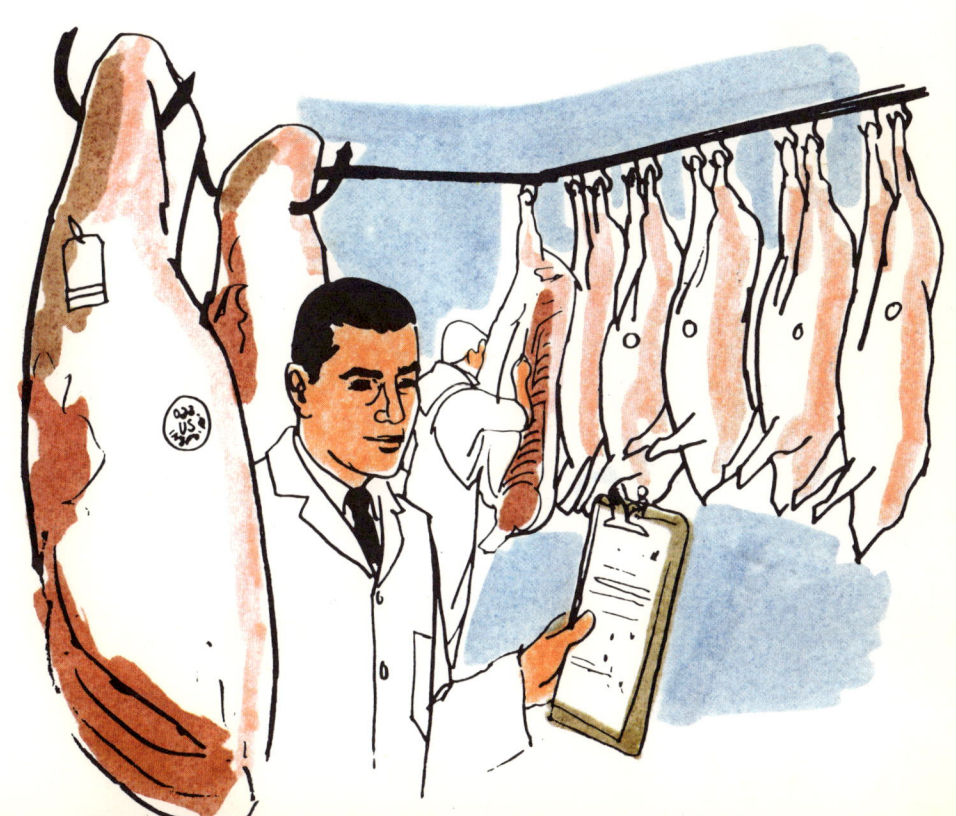

When Grandfather visits, he tells Tina and Ben about what he did when he was a boy.
"We didn't have supermarkets then," he says.
"Mother went to many stores to buy food. She went to the butcher shop for meat.

She went to the grocery for flour and sugar.
She went to the bakery for bread and rolls.
Sometimes she bought bananas from a
fruit peddler right on the street."
"What store did you like best?" Tina teases.
"The candy store," Grandfather says and smiles.

"I like to buy candy," Ben says, "but I like to buy spaghetti and tortillas, too."
"That's another way things have changed," says Grandfather. "You like to try food cooked as it is in another country. You see something different on TV, and you want to try it."

Ben and Tina don't have to go to Italy or China or Mexico or a far-off island to eat the foods children there like.
They can eat the same thing at home.
Each country has its own special dishes.
It's fun to eat them.
"But I still like Pete's hamburgers," Ben says.

Many foods are grown near home.
But other foods come from far away.
Pineapples come from Hawaii.
Olives come from Spain.
Cheese comes from Switzerland.
Tea comes from India.

On the deep oceans, men in fishing boats catch tuna.
Sometimes the fish are canned right on the ships.
It takes workers in many lands to keep supermarkets filled.

Ben and Tina like bananas.
But bananas grow only in hot jungles.
When the bananas are still green,
men pick the heavy bunches.
Other men carry the bananas to ships.
Ships carry the bananas to our country.
Trains and trucks carry the bananas
to city markets.
There the bananas are put in warm rooms
to ripen and turn a green-gold yellow.

How many workers it has taken
to get bananas to the supermarket
where Ben and Tina go!

Foods from near and far—how good they look at lunchtime!
Ben has a hard time choosing what he wants.
Just ice cream and cookies won't do.
He needs the right kind of food to run and play, to grow and be healthy.
People who plan the school lunch know this and help children choose wisely.

Everybody needs food every day.
At home, at school, at work, there must be time to eat.
People eat on trains, ships, and planes.
Special workers everywhere are busy getting food ready and serving it.

Everyone must eat to live and grow,
to be strong and healthy.
Many people in many places work to make
   millions of breakfasts,
      millions of lunches,
         millions of dinners,
and picnics, too!